This book belongs to:

delanex.

ENDORSEMENTS

"Rosanne Tersigni's ebullience shines in her groundbreaking early childhood storybook *We Love One Another*. Eloquently and simply, Rosanne makes the concept of love tangible. In the end, we are all more similar than we are different. This book deftly celebrates that oneness with young children...a 'must read' first book."

—Pam Wong, Board Chair, Congregation of St. Joseph Ministries; Vice President, Strategic Initiatives, Sky Communications, Inc.

•••••

"*We Love One Another* is a beautiful book written in a simple yet powerful way. It encourages children to cherish their differences and appreciate what they have in common. As they grow older, may this book remain in their hearts and may they remember that loving one another creates a better world."

—Patricia Patton, PhD, corporate executive coach

•••••

"As I read Rosanne's book, *We Love One Another*, multiple times, I could not help but think about how her message and story embodies Nelson Mandela's quote for children and adults... 'No one is born hating another person because of the color of his skin, or his background, or his religion. People must learn to hate, and if they can learn to hate, they can be taught to love, for love comes more naturally to the human heart than its opposite.' *We Love One Another* is an excellent book teaching children and adults to love."

—Perry Rhue, PCC, CPCC, founder & success coach, Ekklesia

•••••

"The author has been very mindful and intentional to consider the need for children to learn to love. As a minister I know this is the key element to shape the mind and character of people as early in life as possible. This book is wonderful for school and home use to teach the principles of love."

—Rev. Dr. Terri Strong, Senior Pastor, St. Paul African Methodist Episcopal Church, South Fulton, TN and author

•••••

"Rosanne Tersigni provides a platform for children to learn about diversity and acceptance and to see our sameness as more powerful than our differences. The message is presented in a colorful layout with a cast of charming characters that should appeal to young readers. This book is a helpful resource for parents and teachers."

—Jill Seyler, design consultant and author

•••••

"I love *We Love One Another* and can't wait to use it in my classroom to show how no matter what, we love one another! This book will be used multiple times in the year to build community and remind students that even though we have our differences and similarities, we are all a part of a fabulous group."

—Maria Cascardo, elementary school educator

•••••

"As parents, sometimes we can't articulate in a child's voice what we want them to know—that God made us all different and He loves all of His creation the same. Rosanne does a brilliant job at opening up a conversation with our children in a fun, engaging, and loving way."

—Alex Miranda, visionary leader, brand expert, serial entrepreneur

We Love One Another

Rosanne Tersigni

Illustrated by Jacob Nicholas

RIVER BIRCH PRESS

Daphne, AL

ISBN 978-1-951561-86-4 (Print)
ISBN 978-1-951561-87-1 (Ebook)
For Worldwide Distribution
Printed in the U.S.A.

River Birch Press
P.O. Box 868, Daphne, AL 36526

Dedication

This book was written for my children and grandchildren, and for all the children...our future generations. You, my dear ones, are the changemakers of your generation. Always continue to change the world with the value of love in your heart—love for one another!

Author's Note

To my treasured readers: This is
a book about love...love for one another.
This book is intended to begin the
conversation of loving one another—
no matter our sameness or our
differences. It is intended to be a
heartfelt book about the wondrous
connection we share as we live this
human experience together.

These are our friends.

White/Caucasian

Hispanic/Latino/Latina

Black/African American

Our color may be
different.

We are all part of the community.

Asian

American Indian or Alaskan Native

Native Hawaiian or Pacific Islander

Multiracial

We are alike.
We are different.
We love one another.

We can all be friends.

Our color may be different. We all belong to the human race.

We are all part of the community.

We are alike.
We are different.
We love one another.

These are our friends.

Apartment

Farmhouse

House

Our spaces may be different.

We are all part of the community.

Shelter

Mobile Home

Townhouse

We are alike.
We are different.
We love one another.

We can all be friends.

Our spaces may be different. We all live someplace.

We are all part of the community.

We are alike.
We are different.
We love one another.

These are our friends.

Christianity

Judaism

Islam

Our beliefs may be different.

We are all part of the community.

Buddhism

Hinduism

Atheism

We are alike.
We are different.
We love one another.

We can all be friends.

Our beliefs
may be different.
We all believe in
something.

We are all part of
the community.

We are alike.
We are different.
We love one another.

Many things about
us are the same.

Some things about
us are different.

We are all part of
the community.

We are alike.
We are different.
We love one another.

We love one another.

We ar

We are

We love o

alike.

ifferent.

e another.

About the Author

 Rosanne Tersigni is a first-generation American and child of Italian immigrants, who has always seen life through a different lens. It shapes how she relates to people and the world. Rosanne's life is dedicated to loving all people—believing together we can make lasting change in the world.

With her passion for children and making the world a better place, Rosanne has written a children's book about love and acceptance…in our sameness and our differences.

If you are interested in continuing the conversation about love and acceptance, email us at info@weloveallpeople.com
Visit our website at https://weloveallpeople.com